Basic Knife Making
From Raw Steel to a Finished Stub Tang Knife

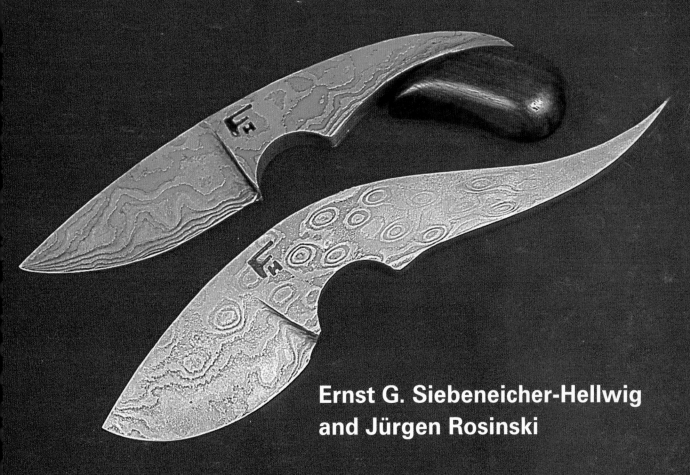

**Ernst G. Siebeneicher-Hellwig
and Jürgen Rosinski**

4880 Lower Valley Road • Atglen, PA 19310

Other Schiffer Books on Related Subjects:

The Lockback Folding Knife: From Design to Completion
    978-0-7643-3509-9, $29.99

Translated from the German by Christine Elliston.

Originally published as *Messer schmieden für Anfänger: Vom rohen Stahl zum fertigen Steckangel-Messer* by Wieland Verlag.

Copyright © 2010 by Schiffer Publishing Ltd.

Library of Congress Control Number: 2009942462

Designed by Stephanie Daugherty
Type set in Dutch809 BT/Zurich BT

ISBN: 978-0-7643-3508-2
Printed in China

Published by Schiffer Publishing, Ltd.
4880 Lower Valley Road
Atglen, PA 19310
Phone: (610) 593-1777; Fax: (610) 593-2002
E-mail: Info@schifferbooks.com

For our complete selection of fine books on this and related subjects, please visit our website at www.schifferbooks.com. You may also write for a free catalog.

This book may be purchased from the publisher. Please try your bookstore first.

We are always looking for people to write books on new and related subjects. If you have an idea for a book, please contact us at proposals@schifferbooks.com

Schiffer Publishing's titles are available at special discounts for bulk purchases for sales promotions or premiums. Special editions, including personalized covers, corporate imprints, and excerpts can be created in large quantities for special needs. For more information, contact the publisher.

Contents

Acknowledgments

Many thanks to Mr. Manfred Ritzer from Karlsfeld, member of the Messer-Arbeitskreis München (Munich Knife Workshop), for his advice and support during the development of this book. His help with the extensive photographs was especially valuable.

Thanks to Hubert Ziegler, M. Eng., for the successful design suggestions and Hans Wagner, master butcher and knife enthusiast, for the culinary accompaniment for the gathering at the Thaldorf bladesmith workshop. The recipe for the roast, which provided the bladesmith and author the necessary energy, is found in the appendix.

Ernst G. Siebeneicher-Hellwig
and Jürgen Rosinski

Introduction

What knife enthusiast has never entertained the idea of making a knife? Many fall short of reaching this goal, however, mostly due to the lack of equipment and know-how. This book provides the beginning bladesmith with a guide to creating a forge, anvil, and other necessary tools simply and inexpensively in a relatively small space.

The book is written so that even an amateur without technical training can produce a presentable result. Of course, you should have certain basic knowledge, such as how to handle a file and a drill before proceeding.

First, we will discuss the necessary theoretical knowledge of forging, suitable steels, and their qualities. With photographs and sketches we will then show how you can forge steel into the desired shape, work it into a blade, and insert it into a handle for a completed knife. Each chapter will focus on the simplest and most practical ways to reach our goal. There are certainly other methods for obtaining similar results, however, presenting all of these would exceed the scope of this book.

Most of the photographs were taken in Jürgen Rosinski's workshop in the former Thaldorf village smithy near Kelheim on the Danube. We procured the tools and materials at a home improvement store and scrap yard in a single morning. That afternoon we set up the forge and anvil, reforged the tongs, and forged the blade. The next day we completed the blade and inserted it into the handle.

In the appendix you will find safety tips, an index of the necessary tools and materials, and photos of various knife designs.

We aim to guide the beginning bladesmith in the hobby of knife making and hope that your work will be crowned with success. If something does not work immediately, do not be discouraged! With a little practice you will succeed.

This book was written with great care, and the techniques described were tested. The authors or publisher and its representatives accept no responsibility for personal injury, property damage, or financial loss.

Important Advice:

Before you begin working, please read the safety precautions in the appendix!

The Theory Of Knife Making

1. Why Forge?

A knife can be filed, ground, or milled from a piece of flat steel. Why then exert such tremendous effort to forge a knife? In addition to nostalgic reasons and possibly reasons that deal with the myth of the forge, there is a tangible, technical reason—a forged blade is stronger than a blade produced by grinding. In the construction of jet engines, for example, highly stressed parts of the turbine are primarily forged. In fact, no other manufacturing technique is allowed for producing the turbine wheels, which must withstand immense force! Only forged materials have the necessary strength. The structure of the grain in these components is highly regulated and can only be achieved by forging, which compresses steel, making the material very strong.

Similarly, grain structure plays an important role when creating a blade. Think of the "grain" in steel as you would the grain in a piece of wood, which gives the wood its strength. If notches interrupt the grain the wood loses its strength and breaks more easily.

During forging, the knife achieves a shape that, with continued working, can no longer be fundamentally interfered with. The structural arrangement will not be disturbed. Sketches in the chapter on forging show this more clearly.

Furthermore, when working with expensive materials, forging is a more efficient and economical way to reshape objects than milling, which, by nature wastes a certain amount of the material.

2. Suitable Steels for Knife Blades

A knife is fundamentally a tool, therefore it requires steel that can be hardened throughout the manufacturing process. To reach the necessary hardness, steel should contain more than 0.5% carbon. Additionally, other alloys, such as chrome, manganese, cobalt, vanadium, or tungsten can be added to steel. These elements produce different characteristics in the steel. Chrome, for example, promotes rust resistance. When the amount of chrome reaches more than 13%, it is considered rustproof steel. The term "rustproof" is misleading when it concerns a knife blade, however, as no hardenable steel is truly rustproof.

If the amount of the alloy elements, excluding carbon, is under 10%, then it is considered low alloy tool steel. The low alloy and pure carbon steels are well suited for forging and are relatively easy to harden in the forge. High alloy tool steels are more problematic because they are more difficult to forge.

Examples For Carbon Steels And Low Alloy Steels

Carbon Steels

Name*	Alloy Element Percentage
C55	0.55% Carbon
C75	0.75% Carbon
C90	0.90% Carbon
C110	1.10% Carbon
C150	1.50% Carbon

Low Alloy Steels

Name	Alloy Element Percentage
60CrV5	0.60% Carbon; 1.20% Chrome; 0.90% Vanadium
90NiV4	0.90% Carbon; 0.75% Nickel; 0.20% Vanadium

* Names according to the German Institute for Standardization.

Furthermore, high alloy steels are more sensitive to forging temperature. The temperature range in which steel can be forged is relatively tight.

3. Spark Testing

If you do not know what is in the steel you are working with, spark testing is the only means to classify the steel without advance metallurgical measuring techniques. To spark test steel, press the metal firmly onto a running grinding wheel or a belt grinder equipped with an abrasive belt. Observe the resulting sparks to determine the elements in the steel. For our purposes it is important to determine if we have simple mild steel, high alloy steel, or carbon steel. Knowing the kind of steel is important because it influences the entire hardening process.

Spark testing is unnecessary if the retailer supplies details on the steel's composition and specifications for heat treatment. However, we are purchasing our steel inexpensively from a scrap dealer. More specifically, we are interested in carbon steels and low alloy steels. Mild steel is excluded because it does not harden. During spark testing, carbon steel forms long, light yellow streams of sparks that branch at the ends to form bursts like a sparkler. Similarly, mild steel forms long, light yellow streams of sparks, but with few bursts. High alloy, corrosion-resistant tool steels (chrome steels) with a high percentage of carbon produce short, red-orange beams with many bursts.

Mild steel with a small percentage of carbon forms long, light-yellow streams of sparks with only a few bursts.

High alloy, corrosion-resistant tool steels (chrome steels) with a high percentage of carbon produce short, red-orange beams with many bursts.

4. Carbon Steel vs. Rustproof Steel?

The debate on which steel is better is as old as rustproof steel itself. Since the development of rustproof tool steels at the beginning of the last century, knife enthusiasts on both sides of the issue dispute which steel is better for a knife blade. Meanwhile, rustproof steel has nearly replaced carbon steel in knife making.

Carbon steel, however, has experienced a rebirth with the rediscovery of Damascus steel. Damascus steel, which is made by forge welding multiple layers together, theoretically cannot be made from rustproof steel. The chrome in rustproof steel reacts quickly with atmospheric oxygen during heat treatment and forms an oxide layer on the surface of the steel that prevents forge welding. Thanks to the pioneering work of Fritz Schneider and Richard Hehn, however, rustproof Damascus steel can be made with a vacuum that prevents the formation of oxide in the manufacturing process. Additionally, several years ago the Swedish company Damasteel introduced rustproof Damascus steel manufactured using a powder metallurgy process.

The serious disadvantage of carbon steel is perfectly obvious—it rusts. This means that it requires care and effort. However, even with "rustproof" steel, proper care is necessary. It certainly can tolerate one night outside in the rain, but prolonged contact with salt water or long periods of time in its sheath without being cleaned can lead to rust.

Even though high alloy steels still require some degree of care, its benefits are very attractive, including toughness, the ability to hold an edge, and corrosion resistance. The price for this, however, is poorer edge retention. Additionally, the cutting edge cannot be finely ground like carbon steel. That means that it is substantially harder to give a blade made from high alloy tool steel a reasonable cutting edge and restore it after intensive use.

Furthermore, a thinly ground cutting edge on knives made of high alloy steel tend to break. The carbon forms very small and hard cementites, which are deposited in the softer iron matrix. Chrome likewise forms a very hard bond with the carbon that is relatively large. Steel consisting of small particles, like carbon steel can be more finely ground than one with a coarser structure.

This is why nearly all of the knives that participants bring to newly popular cutting competitions in the United States are forged from carbon steel. At these events, participants and their knives compete in various disciplines. Events include slicing through loosely hanging ropes, cutting through multiple plastic bottles filled with water, and chopping through wooden beams.

With some care you can prevent carbon steel from rusting. In addition to cleaning the blade after use and taking care of it with oil, polishing it can reduce the blade's susceptibility to rust. Tactical knives made of carbon steel for the military and special police units are partly coated with Teflon and other materials to improve corrosion prevention and eliminate disruptive reflections.

An interesting and unexpected technique for surface protection is finishing a blade with mustard. You are reading correctly. Mustard is not only a delicious condiment for sausages and

Mustard finish: degrease the blade well with alcohol or acetone and dab the mustard on with your fingertip.

other meat products, it can also reduce the rust susceptibility of carbon steel. The acid in the mustard attacks the surface of the steel and forms a chemical bond with the iron. This layer protects the steel in a way similar to bluing and creates an interesting pattern.

It is very simple to use a mustard finish. After the blade is degreased well with alcohol or acetone, dab the mustard on the blade evenly with your fingertip. Let the mustard dry for a few hours, wash off the excess, and then oil the knife. The treated steel should be discolored.

5. Fuel for the Forge

The modern bladesmith uses smithing coal, or hard coal obtained by mining. For over thousands of years humans have used charcoal to smelt metals. For our forging purposes we will employ this ancestral fuel. With a sufficient supply of oxygen, a charcoal fire can heat the steel to forging temperature. Hard coal burns longer due to the higher energy density but has disadvantages for the amateur bladesmith, including producing a strong odor. Furthermore, hard coal is not available in every supermarket.

Very little is required for forging: a forge, an anvil, a hammer, and tongs. Hammers and tongs can be found in any home improvement store. It is more difficult to find the anvil and forge. There are certainly specialty stores for forging accessories, but for professional equipment, you must dig deep into your pocket. Our goal is to spend no more than $30 for the forge and anvil.

On the following pages we show how to assemble a fully functional forge simply and inexpensively in a relatively small space using tools and materials from a scrap yard and a home improvement store.

Explanation Of Terms

Damascus Steel
Steel that is manufactured by welding multiple layers of various steels together in the fire. Patterns can be etched on the surface of the steel.

Forge Welding
An ancient technique that, among other things, is used to make Damascus steel. Pieces of steel are heated to a white heat and then welded together by hammer blows on the anvil.

Powder-Metallurgy Steel
In this process high alloy steel in a molten state is forced through a nozzle and thereby atomized. The powder obtained is compressed in a hot but non-molten state under immense pressure.

The blade with the complete mustard finish. The forging skin was left on the upper section of the blade. This also protects it from oxidation.

The Practice of Knife Making

6. Tool Making

Forging cannot happen without fire. But forging is not that simple in times when we hardly have any contact with open fire. To kindle and maintain the fire, a forge is required. From a hole in the ground with ventilation to the mobile forge to modern gas ovens there are many ways to maintain a forging fire.

Because the beginner normally does not have a bladesmith's forge or gas oven at their disposal, we will build a forge. The cost for all of the forging equipment, except for the hairdryer and air pump, is between $30 and $45.

The old forge in the Thaldorf village bladesmith workshop.

A modern gas oven with two burners.

A glimpse into the "hellfire" of the gas oven.

6.1 Constructing a Brick Forge

The forge made of bricks presented here has some advantages. The materials are easy to acquire and inexpensive, the setup does not take long, and after dismantling the forge the materials are easily stored. With the option of a mechanical pump you are free from needing a power source.

The completed brick forge: simple in construction, inexpensive in material.

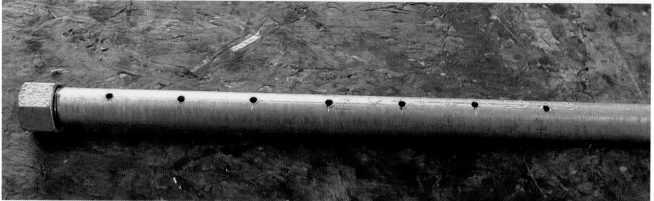

The air pipe: before drilling, the holes are center punched. (Below) The finished pipe with the air holes and the plug screwed on.

The Air Pipe

The first component for the forge is an air pipe, which you will use to stoke the fire in the forge and reach the necessary temperature. For this air pipe you can use a water pipe with a threaded plug (see list of materials).

Starting from the threaded end of the pipe, mark the pipe every 1 $\frac{1}{2}$" along a 12" span of the pipe (see photograph). Then, with a strike of the hammer, center punch the metal at the marked locations. Center punching keeps the drill from wandering and ensures the hole is drilled accurately.

Next, clamp the pipe into a vise and put on your safety glasses. Before drilling, make sure you have a sufficient cooling method for the bit, for example, a brush dipped in water. Your drill bits will thank you by lasting longer and maintaining their sharpness.

Then, using a $\frac{5}{64}$" steel drill bit, drill lightly at the center-punched locations. Complete the hole with a $\frac{3}{16}$" bit. Use the following revolutions per minute for the respective bits:

- $\frac{5}{64}$" bit: approximately 800 revolutions per minute
- $\frac{3}{16}$" bit: approximately 400 revolutions per minute

Finally, screw on the plug and the air pipe is complete.

List Of Materials

- 2 bricks: 9" x 4 $\frac{1}{4}$" x 4 $\frac{1}{4}$"
- 4 bricks: 14 $\frac{1}{2}$" x 9 $\frac{1}{2}$" x 4 $\frac{1}{4}$"
- 1 threaded water pipe, ¾", 31 $\frac{1}{2}$" long
- 1 threaded plug, matching the water pipe
- 2 hose clip matching the ¾" pipe
- 1 used bicycle tube

The Coal Bin

Place the small bricks parallel to each other, approximately 18" apart. Lean two of the larger bricks on the small bricks.

Now, stand another large brick adjacent to the leaning bricks to form the front wall of the forge. Mark a hole for the air pipe on this brick. Using a masonry drill bit (3/4"), drill a hole for the air pipe. If necessary, the hole can be carefully chiseled out.

Insert the air pipe into the hole in the brick and then place the remaining large brick on the opposite side of the leaning bricks to complete the forge.

An advantage of this type of forge is that it can be expanded for making longer pieces like swords. Simply add an additional row of bricks and make a longer air pipe.

List Of Tools And Supplies

- Screwdriver
- Chisel
- Pencil
- Drill press
- Steel drill bits ($5/64$" and $3/16$")
- Hand drill
- Masonry drill bit ($3/4$")
- Folding ruler
- Center punch
- Hammer

First, place the two small bricks parallel to each other, approximately 18" apart.

Then, place two large bricks in a v-shape on the smaller bricks.

Finally, the remaining bricks are simply placed against the front and back of the forge.

Mark a hole for the air pipe on the large brick that forms the front wall of the forge.

With a 3/4" masonry drill bit, drill a hole for the air pipe. If necessary, the hole can be carefully chiseled out.

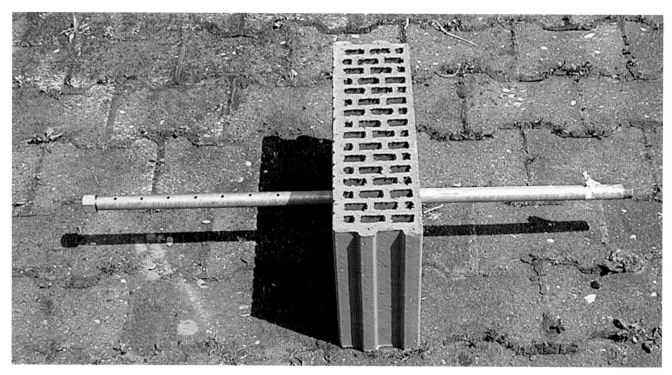

Here the pipe is shown placed in the front wall of the forge.

The completed forge ready to be kindled.

An Oxygen Source

To produce forging temperatures of 1500°F to 2012°F we need a source of oxygen. For this you can use a hair dryer or large air pump.

First, attach a bicycle tube cut to 11 ³/₄″ long to the air pipe with a hose clip. Then, simply place the tube over the hair dryer's blower. Older hair dryers with small air outlets are especially suitable. Thicker outlet pipes can also be attached thanks to the flexibility of the rubber tube. It is important that the hair dryer has adjustable settings. Otherwise the hair dryer will overheat and shut off repeatedly.

While a hair dryer presents the most convenient solution, a hand or foot pump used for inflating rafts does not require a power source.

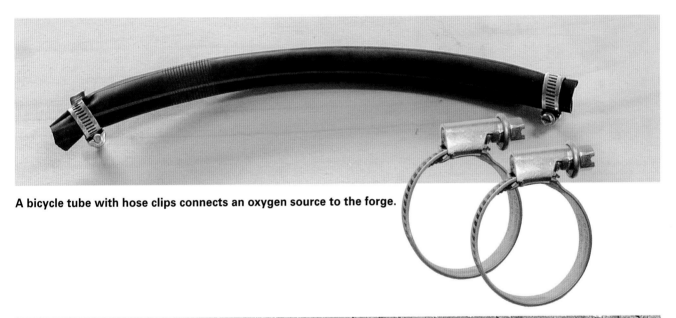

A bicycle tube with hose clips connects an oxygen source to the forge.

Use the bicycle tube to connect a hair dryer to the pipe.

A simple hand pump also serves as suitable oxygen source for our improvised forge.

Ignition of the forge

Fill the forge with a sufficient amount of charcoal and ignite it like a barbeque grill. Common fire starting aids from any home improvement store are well suited for this. Turn on the hairdryer when the first flames shoot out from the charcoal. After a few minutes the fire will grow and you can start heating the steel.

6.2 Constructing a Barbeque Grill Forge

For forging smaller parts, a cast-iron barbeque grill from a home improvement store or supermarket can easily be rebuilt into a forge. The cost for the necessary materials is under $30. The oxygen supply for this type of forge is the same as the brick forge in the previous chapter.

To connect the air pipe, however, you will have to enlarge the existing opening on the grill with a file. Place the pipe into the cast-iron base and coat with a fireproof sealing putty.

List Of Materials

- 1 water pipe, ¾", 7 ¾" long
- 1 elbow connector, ¾"
- Fireproof sealing putty
- Cast-iron grill

Manfred Ritzer, the "inventor" of the forging grill at work.

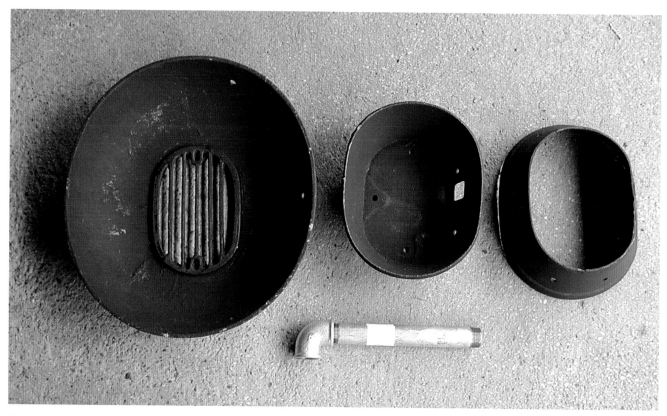

The individual parts of the barbeque grill with air pipe and elbow connector.

Filing the opening for the air pipe.

The air pipe in position.

List Of Tools And Supplies

- 1 half round file
- Brush
- Screwdriver

Coating the pipe with fireproof sealing putty.

The sealed air pipe.

Screwing the upper and lower sections together.

The air pipe, ready for action.

Our completed barbeque forge.

The charcoal is ignited and the hairdryer is connected.

The heat is right...

As one can see in the color of the work piece.

6.3 Procuring an Anvil

The scrap yard is a treasure trove for "anvils" that are suitable for beginning forging efforts. You can find pieces of steel that are certainly massive but others that can support forging. In our case, we chose a heavy I-beam for $12.

As a base for the anvil, sections of logs, sawhorses, a stack of bricks, or a picnic table bench are suitable. Don't worry; the picnic table bench will not collapse under the force of the hammer blows. The pressure spreads over the surface of the anvil so as not to damage your supporting structure.

6.4 Making a Forging Hammer

It is not absolutely necessary to have the perfect hammer for your first forged knife. Nevertheless, we will describe how to make one because we hope that you will remain true to forging. We have adjusted a simple hammer from the home improvement store to suit our needs.

The makeshift anvil rests on a strong wooden box.

List Of Tools And Supplies

- Belt grinder or bench grinder
- Pencil
- Folding ruler
- Hacksaw
- 3 lb Hammer

Compare: Hammer from the home improvement store (left) and the reworked forging hammer (right).

Explanation Of Terms

Face: The face of the hammer is the flat area of the hammer's head.

Peen: The peen is the tapered area of the hammer's head.

Bench Grinder: A bench grinder is a fast running motor with two grinding wheels.

For forging it is important that the face of the hammer is somewhat rounded at the corners and edges. This will prevent defects from emerging on the piece being forged if the hammer strikes at an angle. The peen should also be smooth and even. These changes can be made on a belt grinder or bench grinder.

The length of the hammer should be fitted to the bladesmith's measurements, fitting into the crook of the arm. Shorten the handle to the correct length with a hacksaw.

6.5 Making Forging Tongs

Now that we have a forge and hammer, we still need forging tongs to complete the basic set of equipment for forging. Special blacksmith's tongs are not required because we have left the bar, from which we will forge the knife, long enough so that the back end functions as a handle. For other forging attempts, one could manage with a standard pipe wrench or pliers.

To make suitable forging tongs, we return to an example from the home improvement store and reforge it. We already have the forge and the anvil.

For forging, the peen is rounded out.

The face is also gently rounded.

The heads of the hammers from the side.

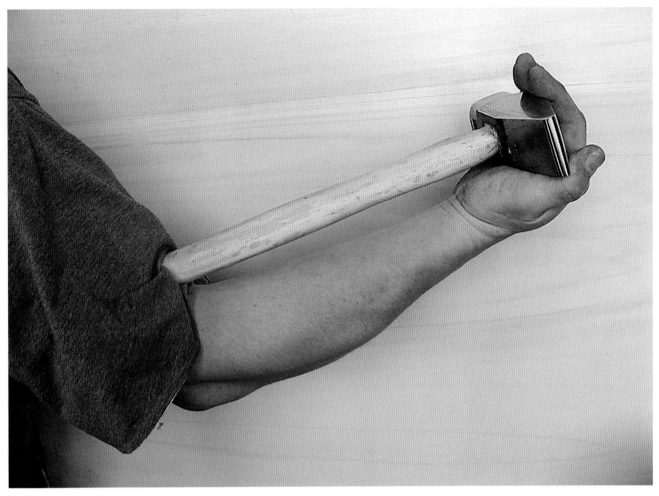

The correct length: The handle should be long enough to reach the crook of the arm.

To reforge the tongs, first, open the jaws of the store-bought tool and then flatten and shape them. The jaws are finished when they are parallel to each other and slightly open. The space between the jaws, therefore, corresponds to the size of steel that the tongs can handle when forging. The professional bladesmith has a number of tongs for various uses and blade sizes. It is a good exercise for each prospective bladesmith to make forging tongs.

6.6 Tool for Forming the Tang

The tang is the shank of the knife, the part that attaches to the material used for the handle. Forming the tang is a forging process during which the steel is clearly reduced at the junction of the blade and tang along the width of the metal. This can be done, as we will later show, on the edge of the anvil. But with a self-made tool it is quicker, simpler, and more exact.

Several tongs used by a professional bladesmith from the Thaldorf village workshop.

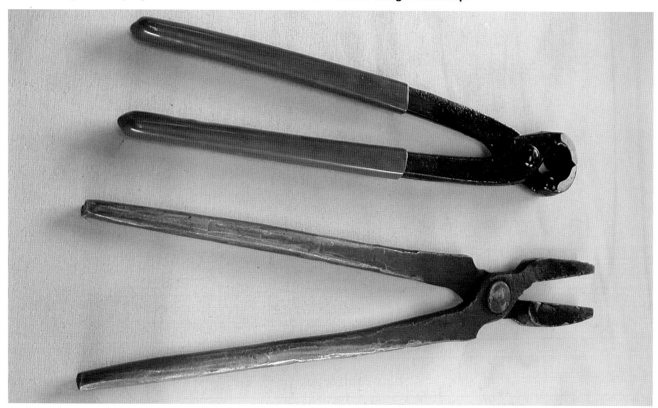

Before and After: Above, tongs from a home improvement store, below the reforged tongs.

The tongs are heated and flattened on our makeshift anvil.

List Of Materials

Spring steel 3/4" round, 15 3/4" long (automobile coil spring, see chapter 2.2.1)

Mild steel, for example St 37, for the base

List Of Tools And Supplies

Electric welding equipment

Forging equipment (forge, anvil, hammer, and tongs)

Tool For Forming The Tang

Material:

Spring steel (automobile coil spring)

Hardened at 1500°F,

Tempered 1 hour at 480°F

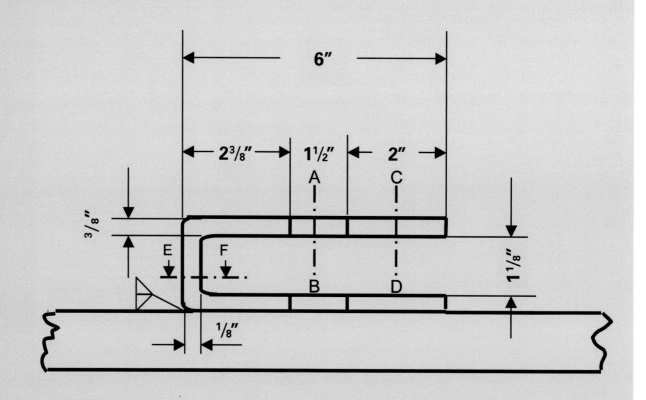

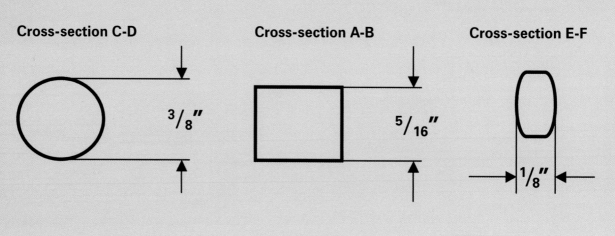

Cross-section C-D $3/8''$

Cross-section A-B $5/16''$

Cross-section E-F $1/8''$

(Sketches are not to scale)

The tool for forming the tang is welded onto the I-beam.

To make the tool that forms the tang we need a piece of round steel, approximately 15 ³/₄″ long, and a base, on which the device is welded. As we will see later in the chapter on forging, we can forge the main element of this tool from an old automobile coil spring.

The sketch shows a square in section A-B. We will make this square by filing.

The round steel in the area of the section E-F is flattened and then bent into shape.

Finally, treat the tool with heat as follows: quench at 1500°F and temper at 480°F for one hour. Weld the section onto the base and the tool is complete.

6.7 Making a Filing Device

To make a filing device you need a good knowledge of metalworking. Nevertheless, we want to show the interested reader what such a device looks like.

Filing Device

Material: Tool Steel, i.e. C50

Small parts: 2 socket screws, M4 x 25

Break edges

Section 1:

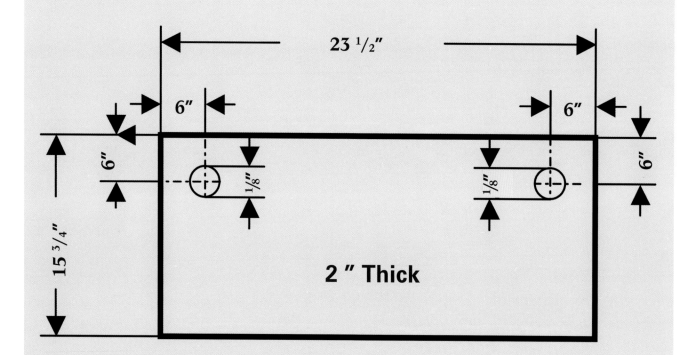

Section 2: Like section 1, instead 1/8" through hole M4 thread.

To complete: Temper both parts and leave at a hardness of 58-60 HRC.

(Sketches are not to scale)

7. Forging a Knife

The beginner bladesmith may initially face some issues procuring materials. Where do I get what? Steel suitable for forging and making knives is easily found at a scrap yard. But how can you determine if the steel at a scrap yard is suitable for a knife? It is easier than you think: automobile coil springs are well suited for making knives. The steel that they are manufactured from contains enough carbon for hardening as well as other alloy elements for toughness, capacity, and flexibility. Additionally, spring steel is easily forged and tolerates mistakes in the forging temperature. The single disadvantage is that it is not corrosion resistant.

7.1 Reforging an Automobile Coil Spring

To forge a blade from an automobile coil spring, the piece must first be fired. For this, we place the coil spring vertically in our brick forge.

A note regarding the photographs on these pages: Because we were forging outdoors in sunlight, the flames are not as visible as in a dark bladesmith's workshop. For this reason, all other elements of the process are easily distinguished.

If the lower section of the coil spring is glowing red, the first coil can be forged on the anvil.

Place the coil spring back into the flame to be heated. Due to its shape it is quite difficult to hold the coil spring with forging tongs alone. Therefore, it is better to hold it with a gloved hand. Before handling the coil spring with a glove, however, be sure to cool the end you're going to hold in water.

Now forge the second coil. It is visible in the photographs how the bladesmith holds the coil spring across the anvil to better forge the curve, and then straightens it out lengthwise.

Our forging work area is ready with a forge, anvil, charcoal, and bucket.

The automobile spring is forged coil by coil.

The end of the coil spring is cooled, the forged section heated and worked further.

The coil spring is forged straight to the last coil.

7.2 Forging a Blade

We have decided on a knife with a stub tang because it is the easiest design for beginning bladesmiths. With a stub tang, the tang disappears into the handle, while with a full tang the tang is covered with two handle scales.

To reach the correct forging temperature we slowly heat the steel, repeatedly turning the metal in the flames until it glows yellow. It can be forged until it glows a dark cherry red.

If the piece becomes too hot in the fire, the carbon burns in the steel, and thus becomes unusable. Steel that is too hot burns white and sparks.

The problem with photographing the forging process is that the brightness of the glowing steel outshines everything, and the outlines are not very visible. To display the process more clearly, we simulated the forging steps on a piece of modeling clay. You will find these photographs at the end of the chapter. We did, however, let the steel cool down partially after the forging process so that we could take useful pictures.

A beautiful stub tang blade made of rust free Damascus steel.

Full tang blade (above) and stub tang blade (below).

Flattening

Flatten the round steel in the front at a length of approximately 3 $\frac{1}{8}$ " and a depth of approximately $\frac{1}{4}$ ". Caution: do not forge too thin in the beginning, further forging will take place.

Forging the Tip

Placing the steel on the end of the anvil and forging a bevel with careful hammer blows forms the tip.

Afterwards, the steel is flattened again. The forging processes must be repeated multiple times in order to produce a beautifully shaped tip.

Naturally, this could be done more easily if the steel were cut diagonally. But by forging the tip we produce a more favorable grain structure that clearly improves the strength of the blade at the tip. Extra strength is added to the tip and the thinner area where the blade tapers to the tip.

Comparison of the Structural Conditions

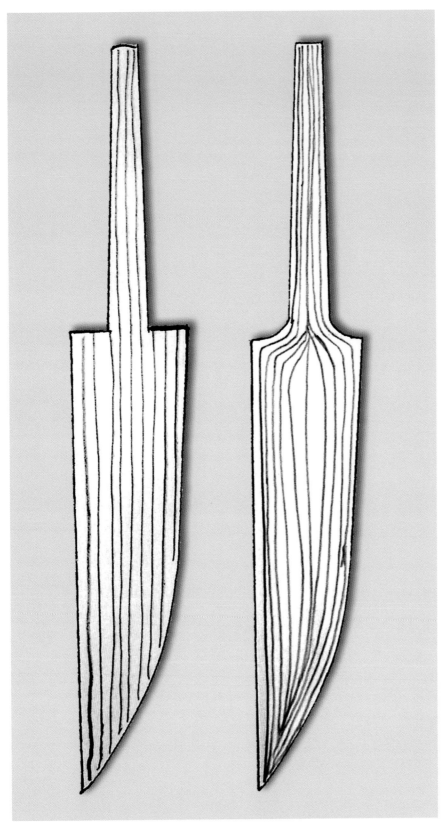

(Left) The broken grain structure of a sawed out blade. (Right) With a forged blade the grain structure follows the outline.

The round bar is flattened in order to maintain the basic outline of the blade.

Then the bar is turned 90 degrees and the tip is forged.

To make the blade into the desired shape, we stretch the blade, which means that the steel is forced into the desired direction with the peen of the hammer and then smoothed again with the face of the hammer.

The shape of the blade is worked out, the cutting area formed by careful hammer blows. The blade is thereby tapered to a cutting edge.

The steel is beaten out with the peen and smoothed to remove traces of the blows from the peen.

Careful blows shape the cutting area.

The blade is tapered to a cutting edge. Its strength is maintained on its spine.

The blade's rough shape is produced without removing any material.

Forming the Tang

Why do we form the tang with so much effort? Why don't we just flatten the area and then saw out the tang? For the same reason we forge the tip—by forging, the grain structure in the steel is uninterrupted. In contrast, through intense forging on the most sensitive location of the knife, the junction of the blade and tang, the compression of the steel offers additional reinforcement.

The anvil's edge can be used to form the tang. In most of the photographs, however, we show how this process takes place with the custom tool we described earlier.

Insert the blade into the tool and make the first notch with light hammer blows on the rounded area of the tool. Insert the blade into the tool again, using the hammer to move the piece into the rounded area of the tool. This deepens the notch.

Then, reforge on the square section of the tool to extend the notch.

The anvil's edge can also be used to form the tang.

With the first notch we set the blade apart from the tang.

Insert the blade into the tool once more with a hammer.

Deepen the notch on the rounded area of the tool.

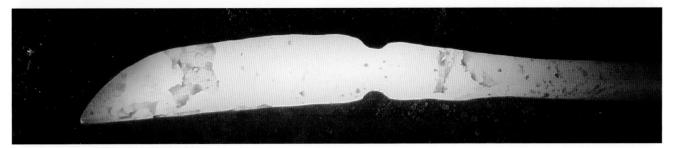

Here are the results of using the round section of the tool.

Reforge on the square section to extend the notch.

Forging the Tang

On the anvil's edge the tang is tapered backward on both sides. In the meantime the blade must be straightened repeatedly.

If you would like to have a tang that screws together with the handle, forge this part round.

The tang is forged and gently tapered backward.

For our knife we leave the tang flat.

The piece is now reheated and straightened.

The tang is completely forged, but remains a part of the bar.

You can mimick the individual steps of forging with modeling clay.

First, flatten the blade.

Next, forge the tip.

Turn the piece 90 degrees and further widen the blade.

As you widen the blade, alternately rework the tip.

The blade gradually forms.

Forge the cutting edge of the blade flatter than at the spine.

Use the hammer peen to stretch the blade out.

Even out the peen marks with the hammer face.

Form the tang on the anvil's edge.

Even out the area of the tang.

With the hammer peen stretch the tang lengthwise.

Slowly bring the tang to its final form.

The result: our model clay knife, completely forged.

Below we will show how to alter a belt grinder from a home improvement store to give your blade its final touches. With this modified belt grinder you can also grind a blade made of flat steel.

Furthermore, we will display how a clamping device secures the blade while you worked on it.

The bladesmith Richard Spitzl at his professional belt grinder.

Improvised: an electric palm sander, clamped upside down in a vise.

8. Modifying a Belt Grinder

One of the final steps to working on your blade is filing it. It is much faster with a belt grinder. A professional belt grinder with speed control costs over $1,500. The advantage of such a device lies in its dimensions. A professional belt grinder has abrasive belts that are more than six feet long. The long belts manage the heat more efficiently, allowing you to run the grinder at high speeds.

In addition to the cost, the size can be a disadvantage for the hobbyist. Who has a workshop that is large enough to accommodate a professional belt grinder? An electric palm sander clamped into a vise will also do. But for making knives a table grinder is more suitable. It is also not as loud as the electric palm sander. The longer abrasive belt and the larger support surface make it easier for working on knives.

A belt grinder from a home improvement store. The opening is already marked.

The only problem is that the blade cannot be properly set on the side because there is no sharp edge on the grinder and no clean junction to grind the ricasso and bevel. A belt grinder from a home improvement store, however, can be altered relatively easily to alleviate this problem. For this, only one opening must be made in the grinder so the blade can be set directly on the sharp edge.

With a felt tip pen, mark a $^3/_4$″ x 2″ rectangle on the grinder. With a hacksaw, saw the vertical markings. The horizontal cuts, however, are not as easy to make. An experienced hobbyist will approach the problem with an angle grinder. Amateurs, however, are advised against this, as working with the angle grinder can be dangerous for an inexperienced user. It is easier to make a row of holes next to each other with a hand drill ($^5/_{32}$″ bit) and cut through the remainder with a chisel.

Mark the rectangle.

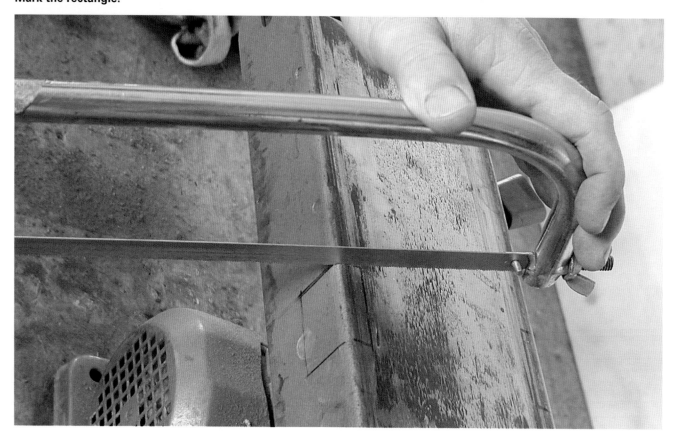

Make the vertical cuts with a regular handsaw.

A rotary tool with a small cut-off wheel makes the horizontal cuts easier.

The cut makes it possible to place the blade directly onto the sharp edge.

Center punch before drilling so that the drill does not wander. Make sure the drilled holes are not placed too close to each other because otherwise the drill will slip into the previously drilled hole. If available, a small rotary tool with a cut-off wheel is also suitable.

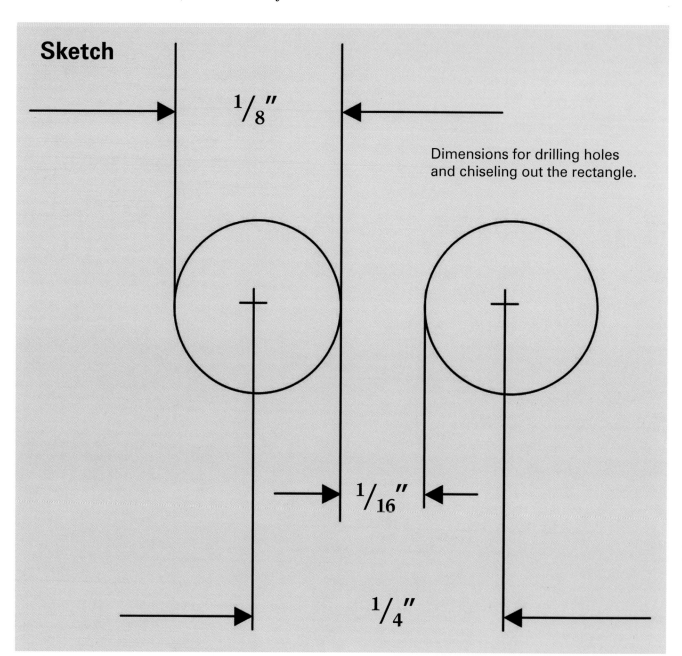

Sketch

$^1/_8''$

Dimensions for drilling holes and chiseling out the rectangle.

$^1/_{16}''$

$^1/_4''$

List Of Tools And Supplies

- Felt tip pen
- Hammer
- Hacksaw
- Chisel

- Drill
- Drill bit ($^5/_{32}''$)
- File
- Ruler

9. Finishing the Blade

The round end on the tang was for demonstration purposes only and was sawed off because we do not have a threaded end planned for our knife.

Before grinding the bevel, the blade must be filed or ground flat on the belt grinder. There is a trick to doing this. To protect fingertips and nails a strong magnet from an old speaker can be used while working on the belt grinder. Use the magnet to hold the blade and then press on the belt grinder.

The forged blade before grinding or filing.

If the blade is level you can make the outer shape of the blade, which consists of the cutting edge, the spine, and the tang. Make sure the tang is tapered backward in order to fit the butt later. Precise filing of the junction of the blade and tang is important as this area rests directly against a guard during assembly.

A filing device that allows you to file the shoulder parallel is very helpful here.

List Of Tools And Supplies

- Metal files
- Magnet from a speaker
- Felt tip pen
- Caliper
- Belt grinder

Use an old speaker magnet to hold the blade on the belt grinder.

Our filing device makes it easy to file the shoulder of the blade accurately.

Explanation Of Terms

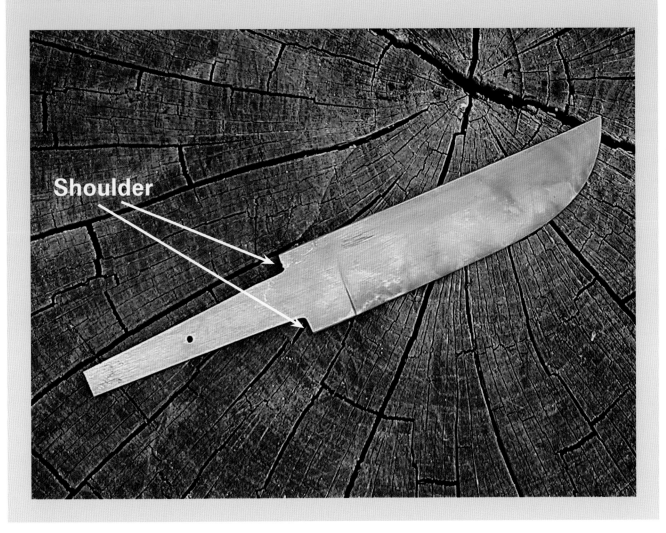

Shoulder

The shoulder must be parallel and at a right angle so that the handle later fits without gaps.

The shoulder must be parallel and at a right angle to the sides of the blade. Exact marking and careful filing is required. Visible gaps between the blade and the handle should be avoided in this area.

Before filing or grinding the bevel it is important to mark the centerline of the cutting area as a guideline. In addition, we measure the strength of the blade with the caliper, set half of the measurement, and tighten the setscrew. Now color in the cutting area with a non-permanent felt tip pen, drag the caliper along the edge and mark a centerline.

Working the bevel finally forms the cutting edge of your knife. Hand file your first blade and then practice on the belt grinder with a few test pieces so as not to ruin your first forged knife. You can also try a combination of methods. Handle the coarse stock removal on the belt grinder and then take care of the intricacies with a file and emery cloth.

Above: grinding the bevel.

Right: Lift and turn the blade to grind the tip of the blade.

The blade is ground flat and the outline marked.

The previously illustrated opening in the belt grinder is very beneficial. Through the opening you can work directly on the edge and produce nice junctions between the cutting edge and tip of your blade. This is the most difficult part to grind. Only practice helps here. We suggest using a file for this process initially and only turning to the belt grinder after practicing with inexpensive flat iron.

If you are up for the challenge of performing this work on the belt grinder, however, you should proceed as follows. When grinding the bevel, as soon as you reach the junction with the tip, lift the blade back somewhat so that the angle becomes steeper. Then turn the blade toward the tip and continue to raise it in circular motions. It sounds complicated but with some practice it is not so difficult. It is important that you grind a smooth junction to the tip.

Make sure that during grinding and filing the cutting edge is not ground too sharply. Leave approximately $1/32''$ on the cutting edge. The blade receives its last grinding only after hardening. If the blade is ground too finely before hardening, the intense heat can trigger damaging alterations to the steel's structure.

Grinding on the belt grinder and filing leave behind traces of treatment that are necessary to remove. To eliminate these marks use an emery cloth from a brand-name manufacturer. Various grits (coarse, medium, and fine) are used at different stages. The higher the grit number, the finer the grit is. For the first grinding process we will use 120 grit. During the finishing process, filing and grinding marks emerge perpendicular to the blade, so we will grind lengthwise to remove traces of the preceding work. For the next cloth there is a 240 and then a 400 grit.

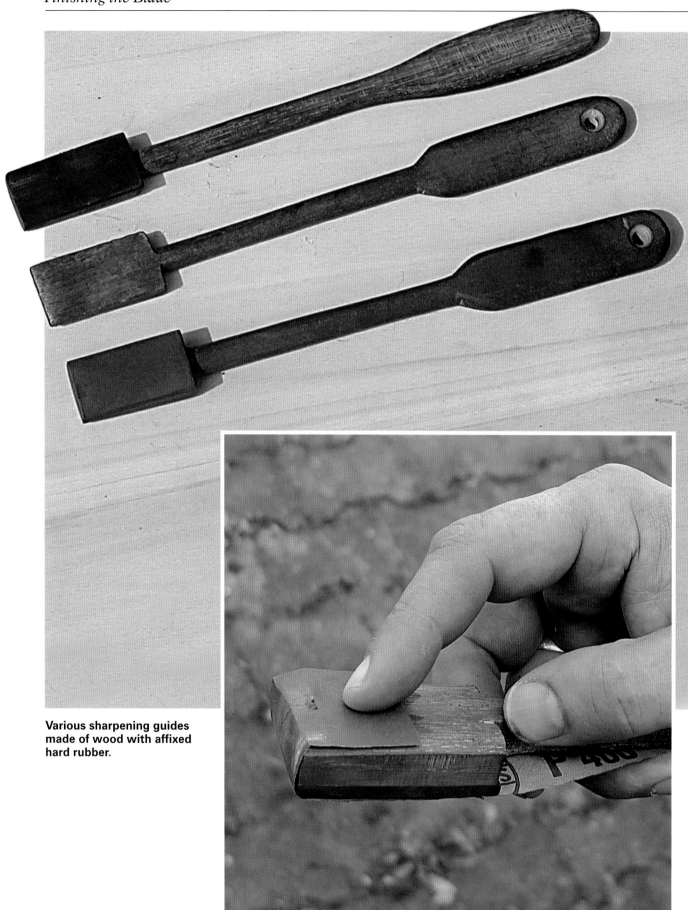

Various sharpening guides made of wood with affixed hard rubber.

Using one hand, lead the sharpening guide while the other hand holds the abrasive cloth.

Unless you want to give your knife a deliberate rustic look, finishing the blade takes a significant amount of time and effort.

In addition to the abovementioned marks, oxide scales will form on the blade when it is hardened in the fire. These must be removed with a coarse cloth. After hardening and tempering you can continue working with 600, 800, and 1000 grit. That can continue up to 2000 grit, after which you can polish the blade on a buffing wheel with a high gloss polish.

We recommend a clean satin finish. Running a 600 cloth over the blade lengthwise will produce this. It is important that the abrasive cloth is laid out evenly. A sharpening guide, as is described below, is very helpful.

To bring the finish to the desired results, you can use a sharpening guide, which protects fingertips and produces a better surface. You can make various sharpening guides by affixing a hard piece of rubber to a wooden handle.

When finishing your blade it is essential to have a well-lit workplace so you can discover fine marks that remain on the blade.

9.1 Making a Holder

Another simple and helpful tool you can make is a holder that you can use while handling the knife in these final steps. A customary vise offers little comfort for completing the knife when working on the sides.

Affix two strips of hard rubber or leather to two small boards and join them together with a piece of leather, like a hinge.

Place your blade in the holder, close it, and clamp it directly to your workbench with a large clamp.

You can make a different type of holder by cutting a slit into a piece of wood with a circular saw. The holder in the photograph measures 2 " x 2 ³/₄ " x 13 ³/₄ " cm and the slit is 7 ⁷/₈ " long. Slide the blade into the slit and close a clamp on the wood. Use a second clamp to hold the wood tight to the workbench.

Explanation Of Terms

Scale is a rough, gray layer of iron oxide that forms on the steel under the effect of heat.

The **buffing wheel** is a disc made of textile layers that are fixed to a motor and used for polishing.

Altered bench grinder with a buffing wheel (left) and a brush for the high gloss finish (right).

A simple knife holder made of two small wooden boards bound with leather.

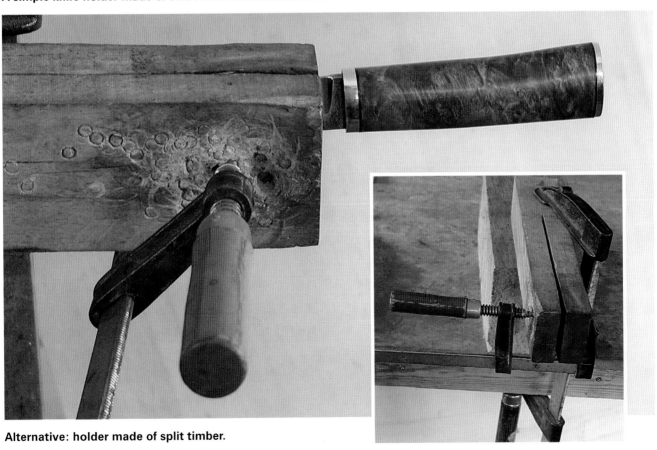

Alternative: holder made of split timber.

10. Heat Treatment

Not until heat treatment does the steel in your knife reach the qualities that we appreciate: hardness, toughness, edge holding ability, flexibility, and corrosion resistance. These qualities are laid out within the steel itself due to its composition. But not until heat treatment are they activated. What happens within the steel during the various processes is so complicated that an explanation would go beyond the scope of this book.

For our project three types of heat treatments are used: annealing, hardening, and tempering.

10.1 Annealing

During the forging process the steel becomes relatively hard. Before any additional work can be done on the blade, such as filing or drilling, you must anneal it.

Place the blade into the forge again and cover it with live coals. After the blade has taken on a light red color, turn off the blower. The blade cools down slowly in the ashes as the forging fire goes out.

10.2 Hardening

Only after grinding the bevel angle, completing the outline, and removing all scratches from the blade's surface can you harden the knife. After the hardening process any traces of work that remain on the blade can only be removed with great effort.

For hardening we need tongs, a forging fire, and a quenchant. The quenchant you use depends on the alloy elements that are present in the steel. High alloy tool steels are quenched in oil and non-alloy steels in water.

Oil is the proper quenchant for our knife. Old motor or hydraulic oil would theoretically be suitable, but it is discouraged because it releases poisonous vapors. An alternative is inexpensive salad oil from the supermarket.

For hardening, the steel is again slowly heated to the hardening temperature and maintained long enough for the steel to be evenly heated. For low alloy carbon steel the hardening temperature is approximately 1470°F. This knowledge means little to us if the temperature cannot be measured. For this, there are two possibilities: First, use a color guide to determine the steel's temperature. When carbon steel and low alloy steel reach hardening temperatures they glow light cherry red. The correct interpretation of the color depends on the lighting conditions. Test the color in a location that is as dark as possible.

Second, steel loses its magnetism temporarily when it reaches the hardening temperature. The combination of both qualities can lead us to a positive outcome. When the steel turns light cherry red, briefly test the knife with a magnet and then place the blade into the salad oil. Once the knife is in the oil, stir the oil so the heat is evenly dispersed. Use at least 4 1/4 cups of oil. A metal container like a coffee can is a suitable container for this process.

Annealing Colors

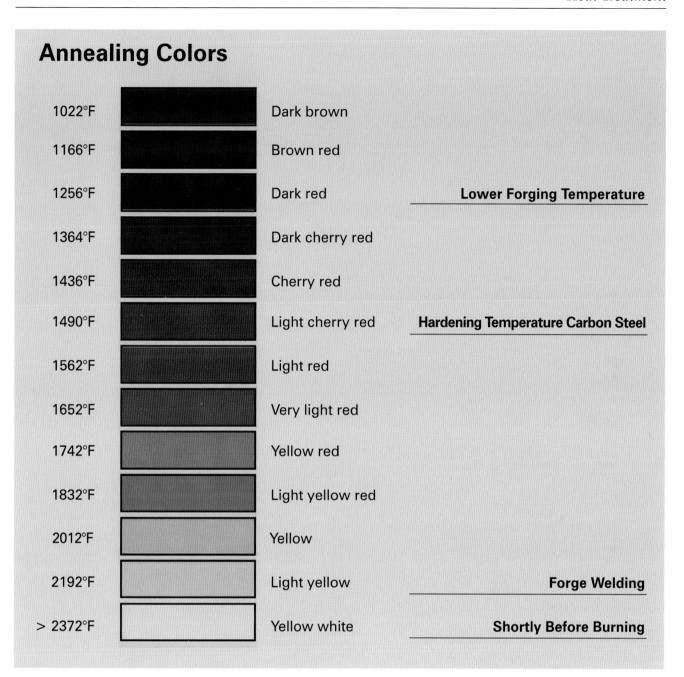

Temperature	Color	
1022°F	Dark brown	
1166°F	Brown red	
1256°F	Dark red	**Lower Forging Temperature**
1364°F	Dark cherry red	
1436°F	Cherry red	
1490°F	Light cherry red	**Hardening Temperature Carbon Steel**
1562°F	Light red	
1652°F	Very light red	
1742°F	Yellow red	
1832°F	Light yellow red	
2012°F	Yellow	
2192°F	Light yellow	**Forge Welding**
> 2372°F	Yellow white	**Shortly Before Burning**

Hardening Temperatures

Low alloy steel: 1472°F

Non-alloy carbon steel: 1454-1544°F

High alloy steels: up to over 1922-2192°F according to type of steel

10.3 Tempering

The blade is much too hard for use after quenching. It would probably break if it fell on a tiled floor. By tempering we will bring the blade back to the proper hardness for use. Tempering allows the blade to become flexible again, yet still maintain its edge holding ability.

The right hardness, according to the type of steel and the intended use for the knife (kitchen knife or hunting knife), is between 56 and 61 Rockwell C. The Rockwell Scale is a unit of measurement that is determined by how deeply a diamond cone can penetrate steel. Without an expensive measuring instrument we must leave at the correct tempering temperature, in our case 392°F, to reach the appropriate hardness. For this we have two aids:

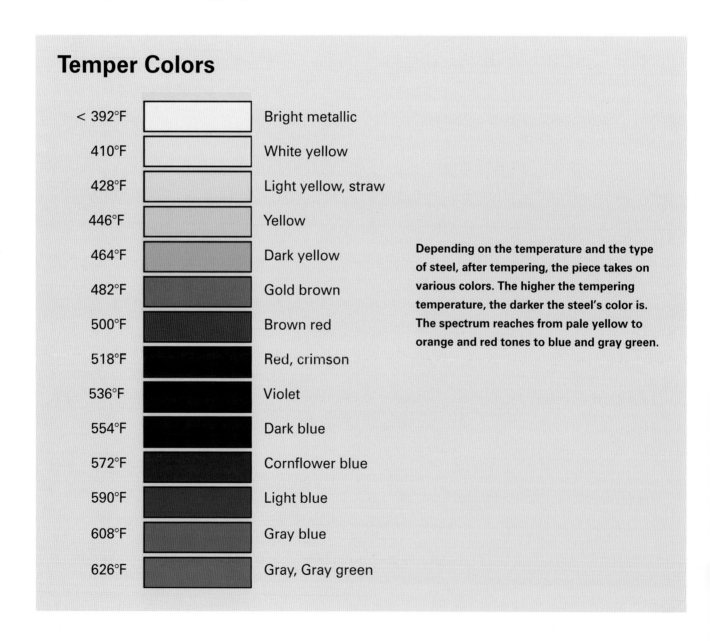

Temper Colors

< 392°F		Bright metallic
410°F		White yellow
428°F		Light yellow, straw
446°F		Yellow
464°F		Dark yellow
482°F		Gold brown
500°F		Brown red
518°F		Red, crimson
536°F		Violet
554°F		Dark blue
572°F		Cornflower blue
590°F		Light blue
608°F		Gray blue
626°F		Gray, Gray green

Depending on the temperature and the type of steel, after tempering, the piece takes on various colors. The higher the tempering temperature, the darker the steel's color is. The spectrum reaches from pale yellow to orange and red tones to blue and gray green.

After tempering the blade has a typical temper color.

1. An electric kitchen stove, which has relatively accurate temperature controls.

2. A guide to temper color.

Temper color changes based on the amount of oxide that forms on the steel during a chemical reaction with atmospheric oxygen. The darker the color, the higher the temperature was and the softer the steel is. The color scale ranges from straw for very hard and to dark blue for soft. A good example for this is a drill bit that is run too quickly and/or without adequate cooling and turns blue. This is a sign that it has become too hot and unusable because the heat has taken the hardness from the drill.

As mentioned previously, the electric stove is the ideal spot for tempering. Heat the blade in the oven at 392°F for one hour. The blade now has a yellow temper color and the correct hardness (58-59 HRC).

Drag a file over the steel with light pressure to make sure the steel is hardened. With hardened steel the file will not affect the surface, but rather glide across to create a noise that sounds like filing glass.

10.4 Creating a Hardening Line (Hamon)

Hardening lines enjoy great popularity, and not only with Japanese cutlery like the Katana and Tanto. Japanese bladesmiths have developed the skill of creating an attractive hardening line to a high art.

A visible hardening line emerges when the cutting edge of the blade is hardened more than the rest of the blade. The harder area appears darker than the other crystalline structure.

A brief digression into metallurgy is necessary. As we have seen, it is necessary to bring steel to a specific temperature to harden it. What happens in the process? If the steel has reached the hardening temperature, a micro-structural formation takes place in the steel that consists of single crystals. When reaching the critical temperature the arrangement of the iron and carbon atoms change in the crystal lattice—now it is stressed. In a stressed condition the steel is hard. If the steel is allowed to cool down slowly, the crystal lattice returns to its original state and the steel loses its hardness. If the steel is cooled quickly by quenching, the stressed structure no longer has time to reform, and the steel remains hard.

During tempering, the steel is reheated. The strain of the steel is thereby softened and loses some hardness.

We will use these qualities of the steel to create various degrees of hardness in the blade. The cutting area of the blade should remain harder than the rest of the blade. With this in mind, the cutting area must cook faster during quenching so that the stressed structure can no longer reform. To obtain various temperatures while the blade is cooling, the section of the blade that should remain relatively soft is coated with a clay mixture made by mixing 100 grams of potter's clay, a tablespoon of finely mashed charcoal, and a tablespoon of iron oxide in water. The mixture should not be too fluid but rather have the consistency of quark. If you prefer not to make the above mixture by hand, fireproof cement for furnace construction also works and is available in most home improvement stores.

The area on which the clay mixture is spread cools off more slowly and becomes softer. In this process a high hardness is reached in the cutting edge while the rest of the blade remains flexible. The Japanese use this process to make Samurai swords because it creates blades that have a hard cutting and are difficult to break.

Continuing our digression into the secrets of this Japanese hardening technique, we will leave our knife project briefly and show how the creation of a hardening line works with a Tanto blade.

After applying the clay mixture and letting it dry for two to three hours the blade is hardened (see chapter 10.2).

After tempering and cleaning the blade, you can clearly see the hardening line by etching it with Iron (III)-Chloride. Clean the blade with acetone and then apply Iron (III)-Chloride with a cotton ball. The steel changes color quite quickly. After five minutes wash the blade off under running water. To neutralize the solution, mix some baking soda with water, apply it to the blade, and wash it off again.

List Of Materials

- Potter's clay
- Iron (III)-Chloride
- Charcoal (or fire clay)
- Baking soda
- Acetone

Schiffer Publishing

Ready to Write a Book?

We're always seeking authors for a wide variety of topics. This is your opportunity to shine! See our website to view an extensive list of our titles. If this idea appeals to you, we'd love to hear from you. Review our book submission guidelines at our website by clicking on the "Submit a Book Proposal" link. Then email your proposal and ideas to **proposals@schifferbooks.com** or write to the attention of **Acquisitions** at the address below. You can also call 610-593-1777 to make an appointment to speak with an editor.

Schiffer Publishing

has books covering a wide variety of interests including:

Antiques, Collectibles, & The Arts

Advertising • Automobilia • Black Collectibles • Breweriana • Ceramics • Clocks • Corkscrews • Decoys • Dolls • Fine Art • Folk Art • Furniture • Graphic Art • Holidays • Hunting • Jewelry • Kitchen • Lighting • Leatherwork • Metalware • Native American Crafts • Nautical • Pinball • Quilts • Rugs • Sports • Teddy Bears • Telephones • Textiles • Toys • Video Games • Vintage Fashion • Watches • Writing Instruments and more.

Design, Lifestyle, & D-I-Y

Architecture • Astrology • Counter Culture • Culinary Arts • Erotica • Interior Design • Kitchens and Baths • Landscaping • Numerology • Paranormal • Pin-Ups • Pop Art • Tarot • Tattooing • Textile Design • UFOs • Witchcraft • Basketry • Beads & Jewelry Making • Carving • Furniture Making • Gourds • Home & Garden • Metalwork • Modeling • Pyrography • Sculpture • Textiles • Weaving • Wood Turning • Tools and more.

Military, Aviation, & Automotive History

WWI & WWII Armor/Aviation: German • U.S. • British • Russian • the Jet Age • Unit Biographies and Autobiographies • Edged Weapons • Firearms • Uniforms and more.

Maritime

Seamanship • Navigation • Ship Management • Towing • Transportation • Boats & Boat Building • Medical • Legal and more.

Regional

History • Children's Books • Architecture • Photography • Landscaping • Paranormal • Souvenir • Guidebooks • Cooking and more.

To learn more, go to **www.schifferbooks.com**
Call 610-593-1777, 8:30a.m.-5:30 p.m. EST
or write to 4880 Lower Valley Road
Atglen, PA 19310 USA
and ask for a free catalog(s).

In the UK and Europe contact
Bushwood Books at 44 (0) 20 8392-8585
info@bushwoodbooks.co.uk

Bookmark printed in China

The clay mixture is spread on the blade in waves with a spatula.

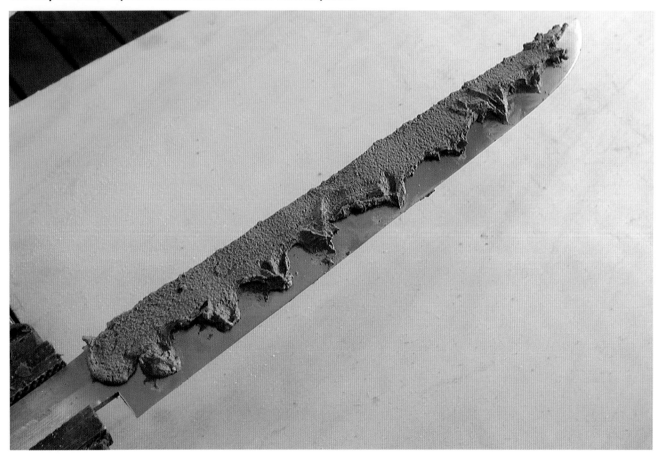

This mixture is only spread on the upper area of the blade, leaving the cutting area free.

After hardening and cleaning the blade the wavy hardening line is recognizable.

Explanation Of Terms

Katana: Sword of the Japanese Samurai.

Tanto: Combat knife of the Samurai.

Scale: Gray flakes of iron oxide that are produced during forging.

Iron (III)-Chloride: An iron-chlorine bond used in circuit board etching, Iron (III)-chloride may be available in specialty electronics stores. The powder is mixed with water, for the mixture ratio read the packaging, otherwise make a saturated solution by adding the powder to water until it no longer dissolves.

11. Signing

A successfully handcrafted work should be given a mark, a signature. The same is true of a knife. We want to present two possibilities here: letter stamping and etching.

11.1 Letter Stamping

For letter stamping, steel letters made from tool steel are available in various sizes. They should be available in a home improvement or tool store.

Lay the blade on a wooden workbench. Place the steel letters on the blade and with a medium hammer strike the head of the stamp strongly. Note: do not tilt the stamp. It is better to practice beforehand on a piece of metal.

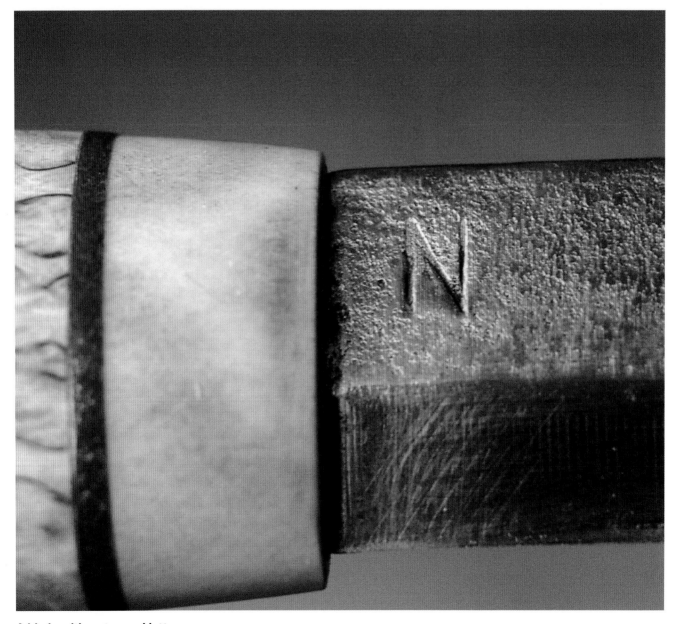

A blade with a stamped letter.

The steel letters are made mirror inverted, which takes getting used to.

11.2 Etching a Signature

For this we need an asphalt varnish, which is used to etch printing plates for copperplate or steel engraving. You can also use scribing lacquer, nail polish, or practically anything else that is an acid resistant coating that scribes well and can be easily removed.

For scribing, any pointed object (i.e. tip of a compass, sewing needle, scriber) is suitable. A pointed brass bar works the best because brass is too soft to cut the steel, thereby preventing unattractive scratches. A brass needle can also be used to remove dried adhesive residue on the blade.

For etching, you can also use an acid etching pen from a specialty store. This pen contains strong acid and is used in industrial manufacturing to sign pieces or tools. Take care when working with an acid etching pen! Do not make it accessible to children, do not breathe in the vapors, and avoid skin contact! Work only in well-ventilated areas.

Here are steps for etching your blade. First, degrease the chosen spot and with a brush apply the etching ground. After it dries, carve in the logo.

Then use a felt tip pen to color over the carved area. During scribing the exposed metal turns to black from contact with the acid. You can determine if the acid has reached all spots and touch up if necessary. After a few minutes wash the acid off under running water and remove the lacquer with brush cleaner or another solvent.

You can also write directly on the steel with a pen. The result is not optimal, as the lines become too thick.

With a little bit of practice presentable logos can be produced. The logos displayed in the pictures do not raise any claims to perfection but are merely examples.

Other options: On the market there are professional etching devices that are not cheap. The purchase is worthwhile only when one regularly has the need. An engraver can also mechanically engrave steel that is not yet hardened.

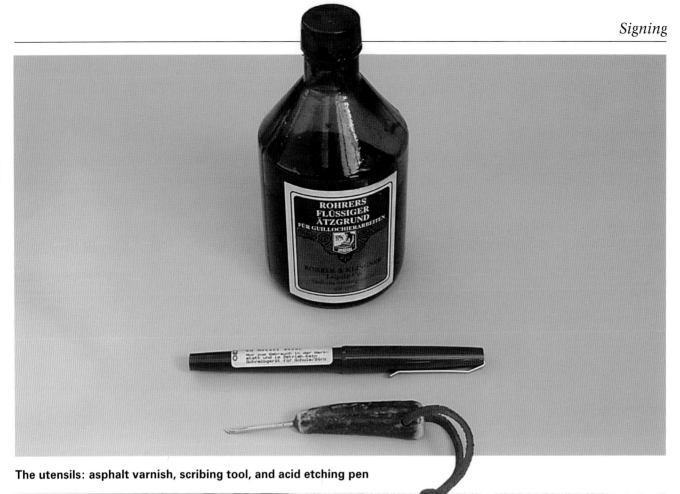

The utensils: asphalt varnish, scribing tool, and acid etching pen

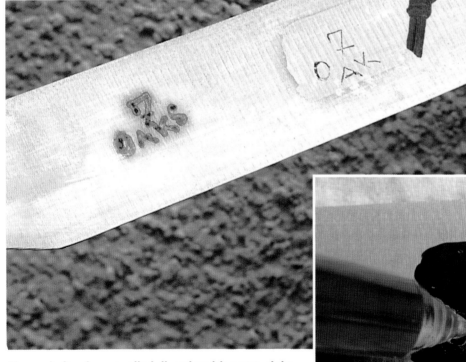

Above: Left, a logo applied directly with a pen, right scribed into etching ground.

Right: The lines are colored in.

12. Knife Construction

After our blade is finished, we can complete the entire knife. We are missing the guard and the handle.

12.1 Making the Guard

The guard visually marks the junction of the blade and the handle and provides the proper alignment of the blade. It can also serve as hand protection, if, for example, the lower section protrudes. For our knife we have taken a piece of nickel silver with a strength of about $^{13}/_{64}$″. Nickel silver should be available in various sizes at hardware supply stores.

Cut off a $1\,^3/_8$″ wide piece with a hacksaw, measure the exact width of the piece, and then mark the vertical and horizontal centerlines.

Next, measure the height of the tang at the junction to the blade and transfer the measurement onto the guard, along the vertical centerline. Then, measure the width of the blade and transfer the measurement onto the nickel silver piece.

List Of Materials

- Nickel silver $^3/_{16}$″ x $^3/_4$″ x $1\,^3/_8$″

List Of Tools And Supplies

- Hacksaw
- Steel drill bit ($^9/_{64}$″)
- Felt tip pen
- Square file
- Caliper
- Flat file

Now we have determined the position of the slot on the guard. To create the opening, make several holes with a drill. For this, use a $^1/_{64}$″ steel drill bit that is somewhat smaller than the intended width of the opening. Center punch the drill holes, as is described in the chapter on modifying the belt grinder, and drill the holes.

Make sure there is sufficient space between the holes, otherwise the drill bit could wander and slide into the preceding hole. Select a smaller drill bit to prevent the slot from being too wide in some places.

After the holes have been drilled, neatly file the slot out. This is a tedious task, but it is worth being meticulous on this step because the exact fit of a guard with the blade is a quality characteristic of a knife. Use a narrow square for filing the slot and a flat file for the sides.

Take the time to test the guard and see how far it slides onto the tang. Having a well-constructed tang that tapers backward helps this process.

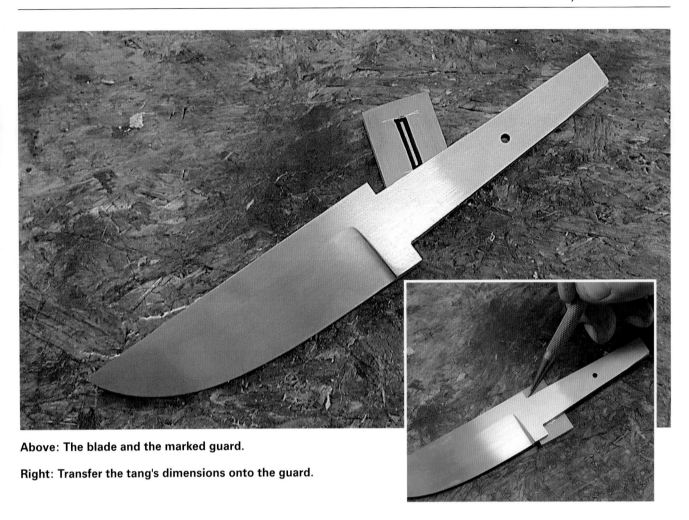

Above: The blade and the marked guard.

Right: Transfer the tang's dimensions onto the guard.

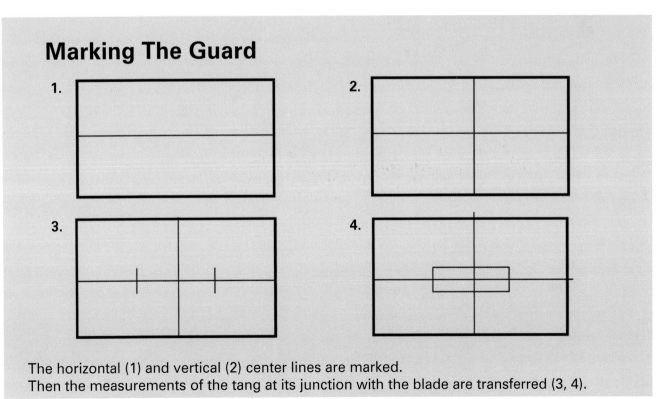

Marking The Guard

1.

2.

3.

4.

The horizontal (1) and vertical (2) center lines are marked.
Then the measurements of the tang at its junction with the blade are transferred (3, 4).

Explanation Of Terms

Nickel Silver: a copper-nickel-zinc alloy with a nickel amount of approximately 20%. Nickel is easy to work with but becomes hot quickly during drilling. Therefore, choose a low revolution setting on the drill and cool the metal well with water.

Center punching the opening in the guard before drilling.

Drilling the holes. With nickel silver use a slow drilling speed.

The slot in the guard should be filed neatly.

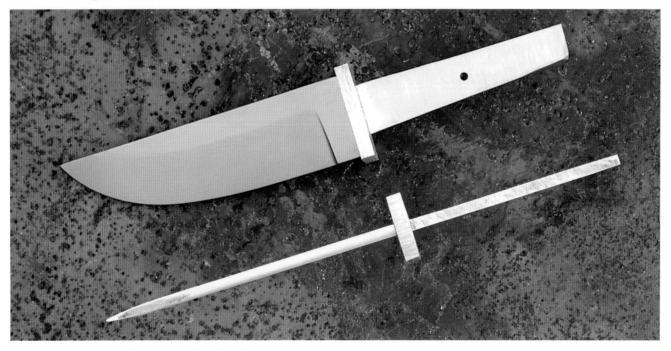

Slide the guard onto the tang to the shoulder.

12.2 Assembling the Handle

For the handle we have chosen a piece of stabilized maple burl. To determine where to drill the holes, we place the blade with the guard on the block of wood and outline the tang. Mark the tang on the opposite side of the wood and indicate the width of the tang on the top, similar to how we measured the guard.

Now make the opening for the tang. Place the wood block in a drill press so that the drill follows the marked line. If a drill press is not available, you can manage with a hand drill. The material between the drill holes can be removed with a jab saw.

The remaining wood can be removed with a drill, like a milling machine.

While working out the slot in the wood, you do not need the same amount of care that you gave the slot in nickel silver because the guard covers the slot in the handle. For this project we glued an intermediate layer made of fiber between the guard and the handle. This fiber aids the appearance of the knife by creating a smooth transition from metal to wood.

List Of Materials

- Wood block for the handle, $^9/_{16}"$ x 1 $^1/_2"$ x 4 $^3/_4"$
- Two-component epoxy
- Adhesive tape

List Of Tools And Supplies

- Felt tip pen
- Jab saw
- Drill press
- Drill
- Wood drill bit ($^3/_{16}"$)

Mark the shape of the tang directly on the wood block.

The tang is outlined on the opposite side of the block and the width of the tang is marked.

Position the wood block in the vise.

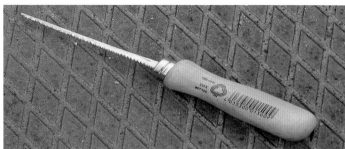

A jab saw.

Using a jab saw to cut a slot out of the drilled holes.

Use a hand drill as a mill if you do not have a drill press.

Fiber also works well on full tang knives as an intermediate layer between the handle and the metal of the tang. The fiber creates a more visually suitable junction, especially with porous materials such as stag horn.

When the slot is complete, assemble all of the parts. Two-component epoxy is good for this. Mix the adhesive according to the instructions, fill the slot, and insert the tang into the guard. Before gluing the tang in place, cover the blade with adhesive tape and let the epoxy dry.

Cover the blade with adhesive tape and glue it into place with epoxy.

93

12.3 Shaping the Handle

To give the handle the desired form, sketch the handle at a scale of 1:1. You can make two photocopies of the sketch, cut out the outline of the handle, and stick it on both sides of the block as a guide.

Now file the handle into the desired form. Make sure to use a metal file on the nickel silver and a wood file on the handle. After filing the handle use a thin strip of sandpaper to remove the filing marks.

Explanation Of Terms

Stabilized wood: Wood is a natural substance that expands and contracts with changes in humidity and temperature. Through stabilization, as the name already indicates, the wood is made stable against environmental conditions. Stability is achieved by filling the pores of the wood with synthetic resin using a vacuum process. Stabilized wood is expensive but the expense is worth it for creating a durable knife.

Fiber: This is not reinforced "fiberglass." It refers to a plastic material with a paper base that was developed in the 19th century. It is also called vulcanized fiber. For example, suitcases were previously made of this, today the material is found predominantly in gaskets and electrical insulation.

Two-component epoxy: glue with an epoxy resin base, consisting of curing and bonding agents. When both components are mixed, the glue cures. There are quick hardening glues and glues with long cure times. The glues with long cure times are preferable because they are stronger.

Pull the sandpaper back and forth over the entire handle. Use an increasingly fine grain to remove all marks.

List Of Tools And Supplies

- Metal file
- Belt grinder (optional)
- Coarse wood file
- Fine wood file
- Sandpaper (coarse, medium, and fine)

Pull the sandpaper over the handle with both hands.

12.4 Polishing the Handle

There are a wide range of methods for finishing your handle. The simplest is a wax polish. You can buy polishing sets at most home improvement stores that include a sisal brush and an abrasive wheel. Hardware supply stores should carry wax polish.

List of Tools and Supplies

- Brush
- Wax polish
- Textile wheel

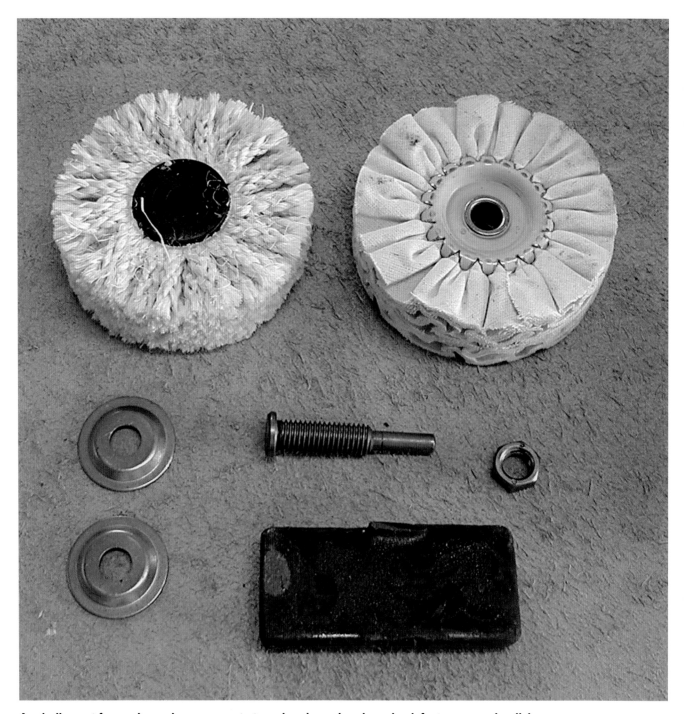

A grinding set from a home improvement store: brushes, abrasive wheel, fasteners, and polish.

Use your drill to polish the handle. Attach the brush to your drill, keeping the wax polish on the brush and then the handle. Then give the handle its last finish on the abrasive wheel.

Handles made of stabilized or laminated woods quickly reach a high gloss polish.

Polishing the handle with an abrasive wheel.

Explanation of Terms

Laminated wood: During the production of laminated wood, thin layers of hardwood with synthetic resin are bonded together under pressure and heat. Laminated wood is easy to work with and easily polished to a high gloss. Like stabilized wood it is not sensitive to changes in humidity and temperature.

12.5 Sharpening the Blade

An entire book on sharpening knife blades would be more sufficient, as there are various methods and tools. The goal of this book, however, is to show the beginning bladesmith the simplest and most effective methods.

The Lansky grinding set is highly recommended for sharpening your new knife. It is easy to use and consistently makes blades very sharp.

With the Lansky system the blade is clamped in a holder while the grindstone is placed over the cutting edge at a pre-determined angle. The angle is maintained throughout the grinding process.

With the Lansky grinding set you can choose between four grinding angles: 30° for a course cutting edge, 25° for an all-round cutting edge, 20° for a wood carving knife, and 17° for a scalpel-like cutting edge.

The standard Lansky comes with three oilstones (coarse, medium, and fine). For domestic use these three stones are sufficient. There are still other grades and diamond-studded grinding tools for use on very hard and wear-resistant blade material, such as steel produced by powder metallurgy.

Place the knife in the clamp and fix the coarse stone to the guide bar. The bar is inserted into the opening for the respective edge angle.

Put a small amount of the provided oil on the stone and start grinding. Pressing lightly, drag the stone along the cutting edge and then make saw-like movements across the stone.

To grind the other side, simply extract the guide bar with the grindstone from the opening, turn the holding clamp with the knife, and insert the guide bar into the opening with the same grinding angle as the previous side.

After grinding the cutting edge into a consistent angle, you can proceed to the stone with the next finest grain. To test your blade, drag your fingertip carefully across the opposite side of the cutting edge. If you feel a burr during this process the cutting edge is finished being ground. In the final step of knife sharpening you will remove this burr.

You can polish this disruptive burr away on a felt wheel. However, using this wheel may make the cutting edge dull again since it presses against the cutting edge, polishing it round.

For the last finish, we nail a leather strap to a roof batten and rub it with metal polish. Smooth the ground blade of the cutting edge along the strap.

Finally, you can check to see if the blade is truly sharp by cutting through a piece of paper. If the blade only catches or doesn't bite through at all, you should repeat your sharpening process.

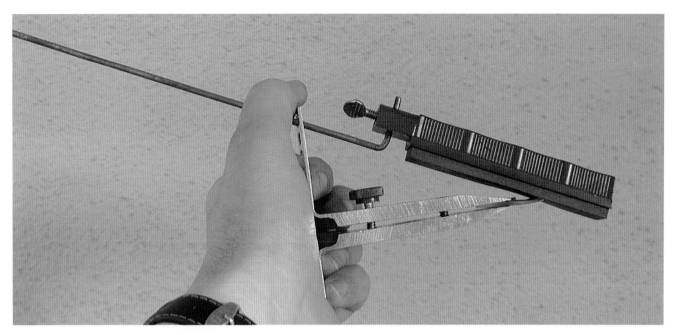

Here the steepest angle is set on the Lansky sharpening device (30° on one side).

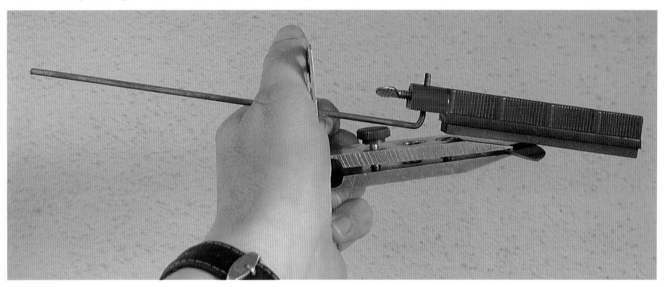

The flattest angle is 17°, which is used for extremely fine cutting.

13. Quality Control

Your first knife may not meet all quality standards. But with knife making, practice is key. Your knives will get better each time. Here are a few suggestions on what to pay attention to:

- Do not leave visible traces that the knife has been worked on (unless you're making a rustic knife).

- Make sure that the junctions from the ricasso to the cutting edge are even on both sides.

- Make sure the blade is straight.

- Do not leave visible gaps between the guard and ricasso.

Appendix

14. Safety Information

The regard for the following information is self-evident, but the truth is doctors and nurses could sing a song about the carelessness of crafters.

- Operate all machines according to their manuals.

- Wear safety glasses.

- Wear ear protection.

- While working on turning machines, do not wear loose clothing or jewelry.

- Only use solvents and acids in well-ventilated areas while wearing protective gloves and safety glasses.

- Wear respiratory protection whenever you are producing particulate matter. The fine dust produced when grinding materials can cause permanent, severe damage to the respiratory system.

- While forging, always wear safety glasses, sturdy shoes (safety shoes if possible), and good clothing (not made of synthetic materials).

- Protect hands with thick gloves.

- Mask the blade with adhesive tape when working on the tang and the handle.

15. Tools and Materials

Complete List of Tools and Supplies

- Screwdriver
- Pencil
- Felt tip pen
- Ruler
- Steel drill bit ($^5/_{64}$", $^9/_{64}$", $^5/_{32}$", and $^3/_{16}$")
- Wood drill bit ($^3/_{16}$")
- Masonry drill bit ($^3/_4$")
- Center punch
- Hammer
- Chisel

- Drill press or drill stand
- Hand drill
- Drill clamp
- Folding ruler
- Caliper
- Hacksaw
- Jab saw
- Various metal files, flat, square and half round
- Coarse wood file
- Fine wood file

- Brush
- Belt grinder or bench grinder
- Sandpaper (coarse, medium, fine)
- Brushes
- Textile wheel
- Polish
- Electric welding equipment (for the tool used for forming the tang)
- Magnet from a speaker

List Of All Materials

Brick Forge:

- 2 bricks: 9" x 4 $^1/_4$" x 4 $^1/_4$"
- 4 bricks: 14 $^1/_2$" x 9 $^1/_2$" x 4 $^1/_4$"
- 1 threaded water pipe, ¾", 31 $^1/_2$" long
- 1 threaded plug, matching the water pipe
- 2 hose clip matching the ¾" pipe
- 1 used bicycle tube

Barbeque Grill Forge:

- 1 water pipe, ¾", 7 ¾" cm long
- 1 elbow connector, ¾"
- Fireproof sealing putty
- Cast-iron grill

Forging Hammer:

- 3 lb hammer

Tool for Forming the Tang:

- Spring steel ¾" round, 15 ¾" long (automobile coil spring, see chapter 2.2.1)
- Mild steel, for example St 37, for the base

Selective Hardening:

- Potter's clay
- Charcoal (or fire clay)
- Iron (III)-Chloride
- Baking soda
- Acetone

Knife Blade:

- Spring steel (old automobile coil spring)

Knife Guard:

- Nickel silver $^3/_{16}$" x $^3/_4$" x 1 $^3/_8$"

Knife Handle:

- Wood block for the handle, $^9/_{16}$" x 1 $^1/_2$" x 4 $^3/_4$"
- Two-component epoxy
- Adhesive tape

16. Various Knife Templates

It is helpful to make a cardboard template of the blade for comparison throughout the bladesmithing process.

The following outlines may help the beginning bladesmith select a knife to make. Hubert Ziegler, M. Eng., from Kelheim provided these templates.

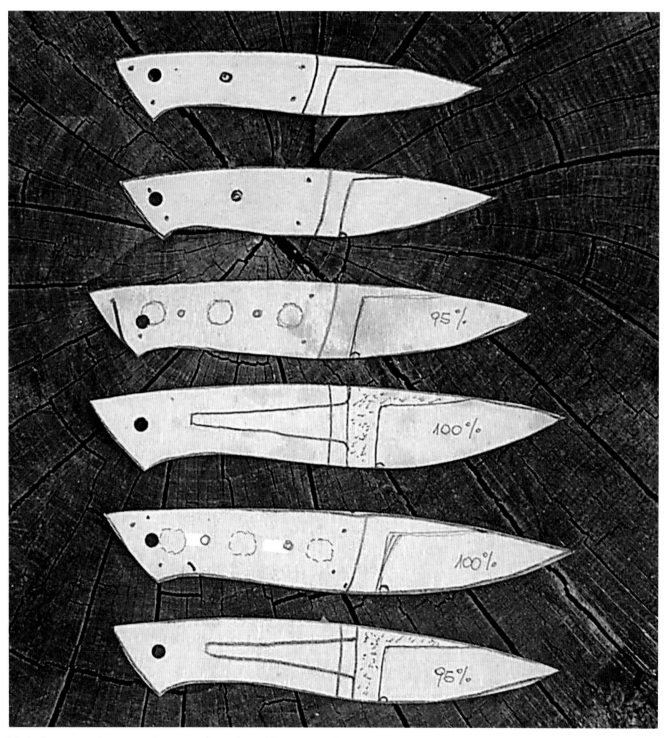

Variations on a theme: various templates for stub tang and full tang knives.

17. Knife Design Gallery

To stimulate your imagination, here are several examples of successful knife designs.

Stub tang knife with a stag horn handle by Hubert Ziegler.

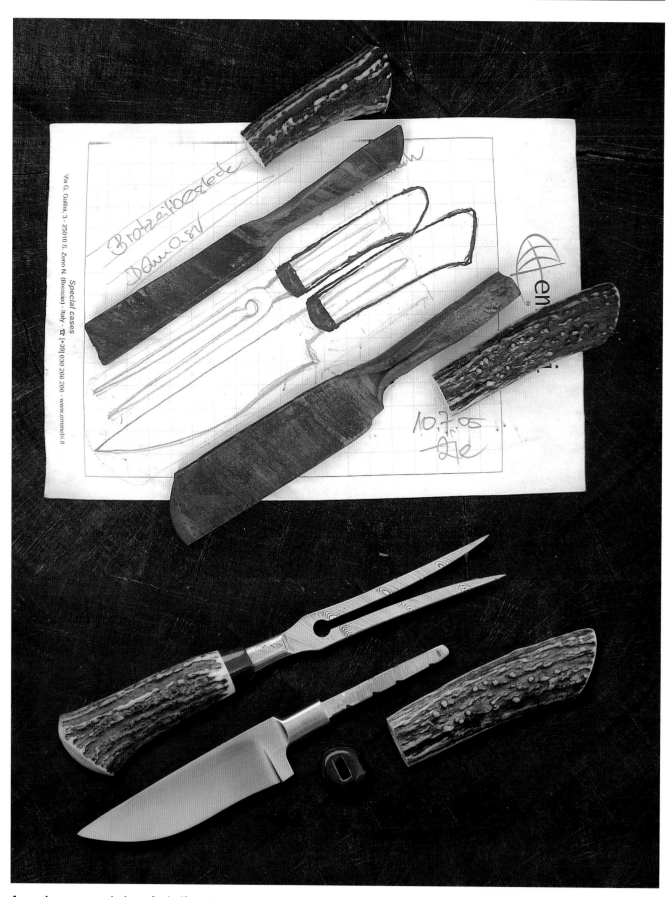

A carving set consisting of a knife and meat fork by Hubert Ziegler.

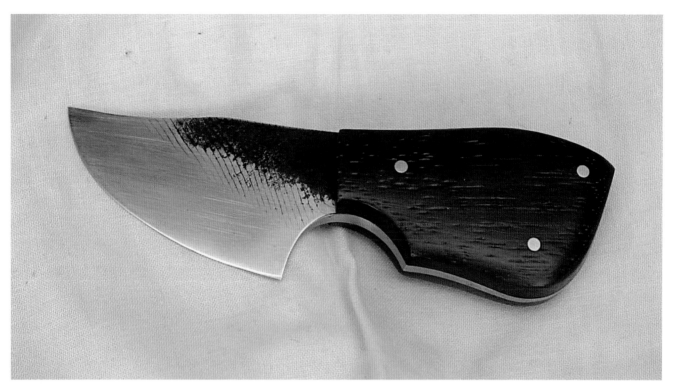

A skinning knife with forging skin left on the blade by Andreas Schweikert.

A Nordic "King's Knife" by Jürgen Rosinski.

A knife by Manfred Ritzer, engraving by Ruth Wichmann.

Two knives with handles made of sambar deer antler by Jürgen Rosinski.

Two hunting knives in Bill Scagel's style forged by Achim Wirtz.

Two knives with forged blades and handles made from fossils by Jürgen Rosinski.

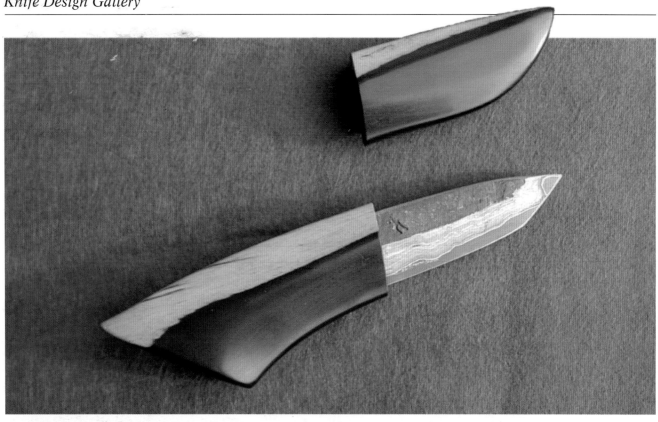

A knife with an uncommon wooden sheath by Robert Kaufmann.

Two rustic work knives forged from an automobile coil spring by Oliver Serniclaes.

Artfully shaped Damascus knife from the Czech bladesmith Filip Horvath.

Ironing knives made from various Damascus steels forged by Vincent Ostradicky.

Hunting knife with Damascus blade and desert ironwood handle by Jürgen Rosinski.

A knife with forging skin on the blade by Jürgen Rosinski.

18. Pork Roast Recipe for Forging

When you have completed all of the work in this book and hold a finished knife in your hands, you have earned a decent meal.

Here is how it is prepared. Obtain de-boned pork rib cut from a butcher. Soak the sliced rolls in milk, adding eggs, caramelized onions, and finely chopped parsley. Season this mixture with salt, pepper, and nutmeg to taste. Fill the rib cut with the mixture. Cut the potatoes in half, the onions into quarters, the leek and carrots into small pieces, and the cloves of garlic in half. Place the vegetables in a cast iron roasting dish (important) and disperse evenly.

Cut the rind of the stuffed rib cut crosswise. Lard with cloves at the cuts. Season the roast with salt, pepper, and caraway and place on the vegetables. Pour on half of the beer and cook covered in the oven at 355°F for 90 minutes. Pour on the rest of the beer and cook for another 15 to 20 minutes. Let simmer in the roasting dish covered for 5 to 10 minutes, then cut into slices and serve with vegetables. Rye bread and beer complete the meal.

Bon appetit!

Hans Wagner
Master butcher, hunter, and knife enthusiast from Kelheim.

List of Tools and Supplies

- Cutting board
- Sharp kitchen knife
- Oven

Ingredients

• Pork rib cut (6-7 ribs)	• Cloves	• Onions
• Pepper	• 1 cup dark beer	• Carrots
• 5 sliced rolls	• Potatoes	• Parsley
• Nutmeg	• 3 eggs	• Garlic
• 1 cup milk	• Leek	• Salt

A decent pork roast provides the needed energy for forging. I hope you like it!